THE
YOU
ARE
Enough
WORKBOOK

THE YOU ARE ENOUGH WORKBOOK

An Hachette UK Company
www.hachette.co.uk

Vie Books, an imprint of Summersdale Publishers
Part of Octopus Publishing Group Limited
Carmelite House
50 Victoria Embankment
LONDON
EC4Y 0DZ
UK

www.summersdale.com

Printed and bound China

ISBN: 978-1-83799-304-8

Substantial discounts on bulk quantities of Summersdale books are available to corporations, professional associations and other organizations. For details contact general enquiries: telephone: +44 (0) 1243 771107 or email: enquiries@summersdale.com.

THE YOU ARE *Enough* WORKBOOK

GENTLE ADVICE AND GUIDED EXERCISES
TO HELP YOU EMBRACE YOUR FLAWS
AND BE HAPPY BEING YOU

CHERYL RICKMAN

CONTENTS

INTRODUCTION

How you see and value yourself, i.e. the lens through which you see who you are and how "enough" you feel, can profoundly affect how you show up in the world. And that can determine your life satisfaction, impact your relationships and affect your achievements. Unfortunately, it's easy to fall into habitual thoughts that can skew your view of you, and lead to self-doubt, self-criticism and feelings of inadequacy.

This is partly due to outdated inner wiring that used to protect us from tribal rejection and potential danger by flagging up our weaknesses and considering what might go wrong. For early humans, our inner critic served as a survival mechanism. Nowadays, it's less useful but is bolstered by the relentlessly high demands from social media and societal "shoulds" about what we should look like, feel like, achieve and do in order to be good enough for social approval. Consequently, we tend to focus on our flaws and what's wrong with us rather than on our strengths and what's right with us. While growth and self-improvement are essential parts of what it means to be human, what we need to flourish in the modern age is to actively counter these natural negative tendencies so we may find a healthier balance. This workbook is here to help.

The good news is, thanks to neuroplasticity, our brains are malleable, so we can remould our mindset to help us not just survive but thrive. We can:

✦ Retrain our brain and reframe our thoughts to be more accurate, flexible and helpful.

✦ Strive for greater balance rather than unachievable perfection.

6

✦ Figure out what matters most and tend to our internal values and desires, rather than external "shoulds", expectations and validation.

By the end of this journal you'll be able to:

✦ Give more airtime to your inner cheerleader than your inner critic.

✦ Counter the natural human negativity bias with an attitude of gratitude.

✦ Replace judgement with curiosity, and swap imposter syndrome and self-comparison for self-acceptance, self-belief and self-compassion.

"Enoughness" is ultimately about finding balance. So, across the pages that follow, you'll find balance between appreciation and aspiration. You'll improve your ability to focus on what's going well and what could go right. This will help counter the human survival tendency to focus on what's going badly or wrong. You'll also find ways to develop more reasonable expectations and set more meaningful intentions that balance gratitude for who you already are and what you already have with who you hope to become. You'll see that, ultimately in doing this ongoing work (which is in constant progress), that is good enough.

It's time to navigate your way through this jumble of judgements, expectations and comparisons to know and believe once and for all that you are enough!

PART ONE

EXPECTATIONS

Expectations can weigh heavily on us. Those instilled by others can leave us wondering whether we measure up and that can get us down. But what if some of those expectations are unreasonable or based on other people's experiences of the world rather than our own? What if they don't take into consideration who you are as an individual? And what would shifting those expectations feel like?

In this section of the journal, you'll define what "enough" looks like to you and explore ways to accept where you are and to move forward with greater understanding about what matters most to you.

You'll evaluate where external expectations have come from and consider their validity, and review what impact they have on you and whether you can set them aside or use them as a positive motivational force.

Expectations can drive us to grow and become our best and most authentic selves, but they can also deflate us and put us under unreasonable pressure to do more, have more, look better, feel better and so on. They can cultivate a culture of "compare and despair" or they can hold us to more reasonable and inspirational standards. Thankfully – as with most things in life – when we review and reflect on them, we can manage expectations in a healthier way.

How you see yourself

In the box below, explore your thoughts and feelings about who you are and where you are today in terms of how "enough" you feel. Consider how you view your personality traits, how you "measure up", your "position" in life and so on. The aim is to shift any thoughts and feelings that don't serve you well and build on those that do by the end of this journal.

How I see me...

_____

_____

_____

_____

_____

_____

_____

_____

_____

_____

_____

Which lens are you looking through?

Evaluate whether the description of yourself that you've written on the previous page is seen through a critical or compassionate lens, from a place of approval and acceptance or a place of disapproval and judgement. Consider why you may be seeing yourself in this way.

_____

_____

_____

_____

_____

_____

_____

_____

_____

_____

_____

_____

_____

_____

_____

_____

_____

Your stories

In what ways do you believe you don't measure up? What kinds of stories do you tell yourself?

_____

_____

_____

_____

_____

_____

Do you find yourself thinking you are "too *this*" or "not *that* enough"? For example, too sensitive, too serious, too big, too small, not fun enough, not dedicated enough, not confident enough?

I sometimes think I'm too ...

_____

_____

_____

I sometimes think I'm not ...

_____

_____

_____ **enough.**

When and where do you find yourself running through those stories the most? Is it after being with certain people? Soon after waking up or before bed? Following social gatherings or after scrolling through social media? Notice when you are most likely to be self-critical rather than self-compassionate and write about it here.

The shackles of "should"

Jot down all the "roles" you have in your life. For example, daughter/son, sibling, parent, spouse, partner, teacher, writer, athlete, musician, carer, activist, feminist and so on.

_____

_____

_____

_____

_____

_____

Write about any expectations (shoulds/shouldn'ts) you've experienced in relation to these roles.

_____

_____

_____

_____

_____

_____

_____

_____

Who is setting these expectations and standards? Parents, siblings, peers, the media?

These "shoulds" come from...

_____

_____

_____

_____

_____

_____

_____

_____

_____

_____

_____

_____

_____

_____

Best life expectations

Which of the following expectations do you have about "living your best life"? Tick those that apply.

To live my best life, I should:

- ⭕ Look amazing
- ⭕ Get good grades in all subjects
- ⭕ Have a successful career
- ⭕ Be excellent at cooking, home care, fixing things
- ⭕ Be loving, kind and caring
- ⭕ Have a fit body/weigh a certain amount/be a certain size
- ⭕ Look young
- ⭕ Have an exciting social life
- ⭕ Be blissfully happy
- ⭕ Be popular
- ⭕ Be adored by my soulmate
- ⭕ Have my own home/car
- ⭕ Love my work
- ⭕ Be fulfilling my life's purpose
- ⭕ Travel the world

The pressure of the perfect "best" life

Use this space to write any other ideas about what the perfect "best" life" looks like and how it is presented in the media or social media, and so on.

Great expectations

What do you expect of yourself? Be as general or as specific as you like and notice the difference between unreasonable expectations and those that can help you grow.

_____

_____

_____

_____

_____

Summarize the expectations you feel most pressured by from page 14.

_____

_____

_____

_____

_____

Circle those expectations listed above that are fair and reasonable.

Put an "X" next to those that are not.

Defining "enough"

Whether or not we feel like we measure up to expectations can affect our self-worth. Yet often our definition of "enough" is defined by others, not us. So, let's explore this further. First, we'll consider a general definition of "enoughness", then we'll delve deeper into having, doing, looking and feeling enough, and explore some proactive ways we can impact these definitions and expectations in a positive way.

What is your definition of "good enough"?

First, what does "good enough" look like for you?

"Good enough" is...

_____

_____

_____

_____

_____

_____

Is this definition of "enough" reasonable or are these expectations too high?

_____

_____

_____

_____

_____

_____

_____

What are your "if onlys"? For example: "If only I was … thinner/fitter/prettier/smarter/richer…" or "If only I could … lose two stone/find my soulmate/become an artist…"

If only...

_____

_____

_____

_____

_____

_____

_____

_____

_____

_____

_____

_____

_____

_____

_____

_____

Beliefs

What negative or limiting comments, thoughts, beliefs or experiences that stem from childhood or the recent past have you internalized? Write below anything that may have led you to the (inaccurate) assumption that you are not enough as you are.

Where did these thoughts and beliefs of inadequacy come from? Who made them? A critical teacher or a family member? Classroom banter? Parents expecting high academic achievement? Airbrushed beauty standards from magazines and media? Relationship ideals presented by family?

_____

_____

_____

_____

_____

_____

Consider reasons *why* these impactful comments were made that has *nothing* to do with you. For example, the critical teacher was in a bad mood; the neglectful parent struggled with their own issues, so a lack of love is more about them than you; the societal "shoulds" exist because the economy benefits when people buy anti-ageing products and so on.

_____

_____

_____

_____

_____

_____

Having enough

With high expectations, define what having enough stuff, money, space and connections would look like if you were living your best possible life. For example, a flash sports car, millions in the bank, a huge house and garden and a holiday home, friends on every continent...

_____

_____

_____

_____

_____

_____

_____

_____

_____

_____

_____

_____

_____

_____

_____

_____

_____

Now write a more reasonable and achievable definition of having enough. For example, a car to get around, a home with some outside space, enough money to pay the bills and go on one holiday per year, a few great friends.

Doing enough

Define what doing enough means to you. For example, getting everything on your to-do list done each day, exercising daily, checking in with family and friends often, contributing to the world, living purposefully and so on.

_____

_____

_____

_____

_____

_____

_____

_____

_____

_____

_____

_____

_____

Now write a reasonable and achievable definition of doing enough. For example, taking one small action towards a work goal every day; completing three tasks on your to-do list each day, exercising a few times per week, seeing family or friends once a fortnight.

_____

_____

_____

_____

_____

_____

_____

_____

_____

_____

_____

_____

_____

_____

Looking good enough

When you think about looking good enough – what does that reasonably look like? For example, hair is clean and brushed, face is clean, clothes are clean and ironed – which might be more reasonable than perfect eyebrows, perfect nails, smooth and sleek hair.

_____

_____

_____

_____

How do you feel about your body?

_____

_____

_____

_____

How does your body serve you? What do you use your legs, arms, stomach for? Is it to look good or are they to walk with, function and hug, digest food?

_____

_____

_____

_____

Rebel against self-criticism

Rebel against the beauty industry that makes billions from our negative opinions about what we look like. Instead – like yourself. Write down three parts of your body that you like – anything from nice-shaped nails to curves or eye colour. It's important that you write something here.

1. _____

2. _____

3. _____

How do you feel about your face?

_____

_____

_____

Write down three things your face does that is incredible. For example, "My eyes enable me to see the beauty of the world."

1. _____

2. _____

3. _____

Reflect on your reflection

Write down some reasons why you like your dearest friends. Is it because they look good? Unlikely! Or is it because of how much they make you laugh, how they make you feel, or because they encourage you or show an interest in you or support you?

_____

_____

_____

_____

_____

_____

Does this shift how you prioritize looks compared to other attributes?

_____

_____

_____

_____

_____

_____

_____

When you think about exercising, getting enough sleep, and making good choices around food and drink, why do you want to make those choices? Is it to do with what you look like, such as your shape or weight, or more about taking care of your body and giving you energy? If the former, how could you address or shift your priorities?

Feeling enough

All feelings are useful and valid; even the more difficult emotions of regret, sadness, disappointment and anger are helpful signals toward the next best action. They show us what matters most, highlight our core values and reveal when and where changes might be necessary. How might this awareness about the importance of *all* feelings shift your expectations about feeling good enough? For example, you might now recognize that it's okay not to feel happy every single day and accept that you will feel low or frustrated or disappointed from time to time.

Write your thoughts on this here. What might your "bad feelings" be signalling? How could you express those feelings to move through them? How do you feel about feeling sad or bad? Are you prepared to accept and allow those feelings, to sit with them and process them? If so, how? By journalling? By confiding in a good friend?

Feeling down

How we feel on a day-to-day basis can generate feelings of inadequacy. For example, if you feel unfulfilled or miserable at work, exhausted or resentful from putting everyone else's needs before your own, this can make you feel like you're not good enough. Write about the common feelings you have that make you feel bad about yourself and/or your life. Remember these feelings are normal and common.

_____

_____

_____

_____

_____

_____

_____

_____

_____

_____

_____

_____

What's behind these feelings? Is there someone in particular who makes you feel this way, or a certain situation that seems to leave you feeling "not enough"?

_____

_____

_____

_____

_____

_____

_____

_____

_____

_____

_____

_____

_____

_____

_____

_____

Feel all the feels

When you're not feeling good, what could you do to honour and express those feelings so you can move through them?

For example, to honour and express my difficult feelings I can: write about what's happening and how I feel about it; cry in the shower; scream into a pillow.

_____

_____

_____

_____

_____

_____

_____

_____

_____

_____

_____

Use this space to express how you're feeling about a current situation you're experiencing.

Uplift list

Could you take some positive action to lift yourself up? Write down what you could do below.

To lift myself up I can: go for a walk, listen to birds singing or a favourite song, dance, call a friend, write a gratitude list.

_____

_____

_____

_____

_____

_____

_____

_____

_____

_____

_____

_____

_____

How else can you create space for some good energy to flow? Which numbing activities could you swap out for more nourishing ones? For example, you might stop watching or listening to the news and use that time to visualize a positive outcome or listen to an uplifting podcast. Jot your ideas below.

_____

_____

_____

_____

_____

_____

_____

_____

_____

_____

_____

_____

_____

_____

Cup-fillers and cup-drainers

On the left-hand side of the page, write down all the things you do that don't make you feel good. For example, drinking alcohol or scrolling social media, binge-watching a TV series. On the right-hand side of the page, write down all the things you do (or could do more of), that nourish rather than numb you, such as reading a good book, going swimming, dancing, walking in nature, singing loudly.

NUMBING ACTIVITIES   **NOURISHING ACTIVITIES**

_____   _____

_____   _____

_____   _____

_____   _____

_____   _____

_____   _____

_____   _____

_____   _____

Now go and put these nourishing activities in the calendar. Do it now before you forget or something else gets in the way.

Give and take

Which people do you aim to please?

_____

_____

_____

_____

_____

_____

_____

What sacrifices do you make to prioritize others?

_____

_____

_____

_____

_____

_____

_____

_____

_____

Reflection time – why does "enoughness" matter?

Why do you think we, as a society, even care about whether we are being/having/doing/looking or feeling good enough? To impress others and prove ourselves? To feel admired and respected? To attract people into our lives? Explore this below.

Now write down other reasons being/having/doing/looking or feeling good enough is important to you. For example, "I feel like my life has meaning if I accomplish things"; "I've always wanted to have my own home because it makes me feel safe and secure"; "Creative and fulfilling work matters to me because I want to enjoy my job" and so on.

What will they think?

Are your desires and aspirations driven by *your* values and core desires or by external expectations and what others might think?

_____

_____

_____

_____

_____

_____

Often we care about our "enoughness" because what other people think of us matters. As explained on the next page, this is an inbuilt human survival instinct to protect us from rejection. But in this case, it's important to remember:

✦ We can't control what other people think of us, only what we think and how we feel about ourselves.

✦ What other people think of us can depend on how they think and feel about themselves, their own self-worth, and their own unique life experiences. It often has nothing to do with us or who we really are at all.

✦ Humans are quite self-absorbed; generally other people are not thinking as much about us as we think they are – they're more likely worrying about what we think of them!

Fear of rejection

Human beings are wired to fear rejection and to seek validation because, in order to survive, early humans needed to belong to a tribe to avoid rejection and ejection from it. This inbuilt fear of rejection (and consequential need for approval) has remained, so it's important to be aware of it so we can effectively manage it. Who do you fear rejection from? Family, friends, workmates or other peers, teachers? What is this fear stopping you from doing? How is it limiting your behaviours?

For example, "I must do/be/have/look/feel this way in order to be accepted and approved of by others."

How do you measure your worth?

Which metrics do you use to measure your "enoughness"? Tick all that apply...

○ Numbers on a weighing scale

○ Number of friends/followers on social media

○ Number of actual friends (IRL)

○ Likes your content gets on social media

○ Grades/marks you get or goals/points you score

○ How much you've accomplished in life

○ How much you've accomplished today

○ How big your accomplishments are

○ Whether you've ticked enough off your to-do list

○ Whether you are being purposeful enough

○ Whether you are contributing enough

○ Whether you are impressing people enough

○ How much money you are earning

○ How happy you feel

○ How you compare with your peers

○ How popular you are

◯ How young you look

◯ How good a parent/sibling/daughter/son/friend you are

◯ How well you do your job

Write down any other metrics you use to measure your "enoughness" below:

_____

_____

_____

_____

_____

_____

_____

_____

_____

_____

_____

New metrics

What matters most to you? For example, health, being of service, being kind, spending time with friends and/or family, learning.

_____

_____

_____

_____

_____

_____

_____

_____

What values do you hold dear? Maybe honesty and integrity are important to you? Or perhaps justice and being treated fairly are crucial? Write your top five values below.

1. _____

2. _____

3. _____

4. _____

5. _____

Success, excellence and happiness aren't the only metrics. What other healthier ways could you use to measure your own worthiness? What different metrics could you put in place? Base these on your values and what matters most to you, for example, whether you've made someone smile/feel better or how kind or helpful, honest or grateful you've been.

Enough redefined

Based on what you've learned from using this workbook so far, use this space to write your new and more reasonable definition of what enough truly is.

I am enough when…

_____

_____

_____

I have enough when…

_____

_____

_____

I look good enough when…

_____

_____

_____

I feel good enough when…

_____

_____

_____

Write down any other thoughts about your newly defined more reasonable and realistic (and achievable) definition of "enoughness" below.

PART TWO

BALANCE

The key to "enoughness" is balance. We can feel good enough and like we have enough when we find sufficient balance between appreciation and achievement, gratitude and growth, and between self-improvement and self-acceptance.

In this section we'll redress the imbalances that external and internal influences can introduce into our lives. First, we'll balance acceptance of our weaknesses with development of our strengths. Then we'll counter-balance our default negativity bias with positive reframes. This will help us to swing the "enoughness" pendulum back to a happier, healthier and more reasonable medium.

A sense of balance helps us to focus on appreciating what we already have and who we already are, along with striving for what we want and who we hope to become.

We'll explore how being your best self all day, every day, is unreasonable and not sustainable, as well as looking at what your authentic self looks like, feels like and accomplishes so you can continue to create a more reasonable definition of what good enough truly is.

Find a balance

The "Worst-Case, Best-Case, Most-Likely-Case Scenario game" helps find a more balanced perspective by imagining the worst-case scenario and attributing a percentage of likelihood to that happening, doing the same with an equally outlandish best-case scenario, before attributing a percentage of likelihood to the most-likely-case scenario happening. This exercise helps to bring our brain back to what is most likely likely and authentic, providing a more balanced perspective. We can do something similar with our thoughts about our "enoughness" to move from best self and worst self to authentic good enough self.

What does your best possible self look like, feel like, have, do, achieve?

_____

_____

_____

_____

_____

What does your worst possible self look like, feel like, have, do, achieve?

_____

_____

_____

_____

_____

What does your authentic real self look like, feel like, have, do, achieve? This will likely be a more achievable and sustainable happy medium between your best and worst self.

_____

_____

_____

_____

_____

Be as you are

How does it make you feel when you consistently don't measure up to being your best possible self?

_____

_____

_____

_____

_____

Is it reasonable to expect to be your best self all the time or is it more reasonable to accept that you will sometimes look a mess, feel a mess and achieve very little? And that's okay?

_____

_____

_____

_____

_____

_____

Fitting in vs belonging

Fitting in is often about being who you think you *should* be in order to please and/or be like other people. Whereas belonging isn't about moulding yourself to fit into someone else's standard or ideal, but about being who you are and feeling accepted.

It's far healthier to change where you spend your time and who you spend time with (to the places that make you feel like you belong and the people who make you feel comfortable) than to change who you are to fit in with people who don't make you feel that sense of belonging.

Where I belong

What do you do in certain environments to "cover up" or hide your true self? For example, you might tone down your accent or your clothing style.

_____

_____

_____

_____

_____

Where or in whose company do you find that you don't need to hide your quirks or tone yourself down or pretend you're less or more than you are? Who makes you feel good about yourself?

_____

_____

_____

_____

_____

_____

_____

List ways you could find your tribe, such as joining groups (online and offline) that share your interests.

_____

_____

_____

_____

_____

_____

_____

_____

_____

_____

_____

_____

_____

_____

_____

_____

Your true self

Find a photograph of yourself as a child. Who were you before the world told you who you *should* be? List all that you were.

_____

_____

_____

_____

_____

_____

Write down all that you are today, including all characteristics "positive" and "negative". For example, are you determined, creative, messy, forgetful, talkative, kind, impatient?

_____

_____

_____

_____

_____

See, honour and celebrate the true parts of you. There is nobody else exactly like you on the planet and that is your power.

If you had the courage to live a life where you are true to yourself, not the life others expected of you, what would you do? Where would you go? How would you show up?

_____

_____

_____

_____

_____

_____

_____

_____

_____

_____

_____

_____

_____

_____

_____

_____

Do what you love

How do you prefer to spend your time? Which activities spark your interest and engage you so much that you can lose track of time when you're immersed in them? What do you like doing if you have some spare time?

_____

_____

_____

_____

What did you used to love doing when you were ten years old?

_____

_____

_____

_____

What activities are non-negotiable parts of your day?

_____

_____

_____

_____

_____

If you only had one week left to live, what would you want to do and with whom?

_____

_____

_____

_____

_____

_____

_____

_____

_____

_____

_____

_____

_____

_____

_____

_____

Love what you do

If you were guaranteed to succeed in any career, what would you try? And, even more importantly, if you were likely to fail, what would you do anyway because you love it so much?

_____

_____

_____

_____

_____

_____

_____

_____

_____

_____

_____

_____

_____

Your cares

What issues do you care most about? For example, you might feel strongly about gender or racial inequality, or about the environment or stopping animal cruelty.

_____

_____

_____

_____

_____

_____

_____

_____

_____

_____

_____

_____

_____

Using your superpowers

What skills do you include on your CV? What else are you good at that isn't listed on your CV? What are your superpowers? For example, you might be a good listener, or you might be good at noticing how others feel or good at getting stuff done. We'll explore your strengths in more detail on pages 80 and 82.

Replace inadequacy with inspiration

Now you've defined what is expected of you and why, what enough looks like for you, who you truly are and where you belong, this will help counter the distorted data from external sources and the swayed biases that skew the stories you tell yourself.

However, our sense of "enoughness" is often determined by how we measure up to others. The problem is we tend to compare our whole selves to other people's partial selves. We can't know what others are truly wrangling with or what keeps them up at night, because we rarely share every single detail with every single person. And even if you do know someone's truth, you never know everything, so it's futile to compare our actual reality with someone else's partial reality. This is especially true on social media, where what we see is curated, filtered and edited.

We will still compare because we are human, but what if we used this default human tendency to our advantage? What if we harnessed comparison and the feelings it brings up – we're looking at you, envy, inadequacy, disappointment – to help us grow and flourish?

By exploring what or who makes us feel envious, disappointed and like we don't measure up in comparison, we can better understand what matters most to us in creating a fulfilling life and set about making the most impactful changes, while also being gentle with ourselves.

We can shift perspective to replace "compare and despair" with "compare and inspire": to be inspired by those who have what we want and generate good energy from those comparisons that motivate us to develop ourselves and our lives in the right direction.

I wonder...

Write a list of comparison "triggers", i.e. the things or attributes other people have that make you feel inadequate, envious, disappointed or inspired.

_____

_____

_____

_____

_____

_____

_____

_____

Look at this list of things other people either have or are that make you feel a certain way and get curious. Consider why these things or attributes matter so much to you. Then ask yourself: what's another way of looking at this?

For example, is a bigger house always better? Doesn't a harmonious home that is warm and cosy matter more? Or if you find yourself negatively comparing your sensitivity to someone else's bold confidence, get curious about what superpowers your sensitivity gives you, such as the capacity to care deeply enough to take action and positively impact the world. Whether you are confident or sensitive there are benefits to being the way you are.

What's another way of looking at this?

What if it's good enough to...

_____

_____

_____

What if it's better to have...

_____

_____

_____

than...

_____

_____

_____

What if it's good enough to be...

_____

_____

What if it's good enough to value...

_____

_____

What do you really want?

What does the insight you've gained about what makes you feel envious and/or inspired reveal about what matters most to you in creating a fulfilling life?

What tiny actions could you take to make changes that will help you achieve or gain what is important to you? For example, drink more water, schedule time in for creative pursuits, book onto a course or workshop, save a certain amount of money each month, update your CV, paint once a month.

Change the way you compare

Comparison is part of human nature. We measure ourselves against others to assess how we're doing, but we can choose what to do with those measurements and use them as a source of feedback and model of what's possible, to help motivate ourselves to learn and grow.

Reframe comparative thoughts below. Ask yourself whether there's another way of seeing this. For example, instead of "They are better than me", how about, "They inspire me to put in more effort."

_____

_____

_____

_____

_____

_____

_____

_____

_____

_____

_____

Choose temporal comparison (where you only compare yourself with yourself) rather than social comparison (where you compare yourself with others).

Write about your own personal journey and your progress. How have you progressed in your career or in your fitness journey, improved a certain skill or reduced anxiety? What small wins can you celebrate today that will motivate you to keep going and keep growing?

_____

_____

_____

_____

_____

_____

_____

_____

_____

_____

_____

_____

_____

Seeing you, seeing me

What is there about you and your life that other people might compare themselves and their lives with? This could be anything from a roof over your head and a supportive relationship to parents who are still alive, the children or pets you are blessed with or workmates you have fun with. Shift the lens to seeing yourself as the inspiration and as a person who has what others might want.

Balance gratitude with growth

The human paradox is that we are good enough as we are because each of us is a unique miracle. Yet humans are also born to develop and grow, which requires ongoing learning and improvement. The key here is to remember that improving yourself doesn't mean you weren't enough *before* you improved. You are enough *and* you can improve.

To cultivate a sense of "enoughness" and abundance rather than focusing on inadequacy and lack, it's important to devote equal time to working on areas of yourself and your life that you want to improve, along with accepting and appreciating who you already are and what you already have. This way you can balance gratitude with growth.

Appreciation – count your blessings

List what you have and are grateful for in your life rather than what you lack.

What are you grateful for in general and why?

_____

_____

_____

_____

_____

_____

Look around you and use your senses of sight, sound, smell, touch and taste. What are you grateful for in the present moment and why?

_____

_____

_____

_____

_____

_____

Who are you grateful for and why?

_____

_____

_____

_____

_____

What places or spaces are you grateful for and why?

_____

_____

_____

_____

What things are you grateful for and why?

_____

_____

_____

_____

Thank yourself

What have *you* done to bring those things/people/events/experiences that you are grateful for into your life? It's time to take some credit for some of the good you have created.

Celebrate your wins

List your achievements. These needn't be huge "big-dream" wins – you can include accomplishments such as helping a friend out, winning a medal at school, becoming a parent and raising a child, getting the job you wanted, leaving a toxic relationship or navigating your way through grief.

_____

_____

_____

_____

_____

_____

Underline those that you haven't yet congratulated yourself for, then go ahead and claim them. Say or write, "I'm proud of myself for..."

_____

_____

_____

_____

_____

_____

See your struggles and strengths

Write about any challenges you've risen to, any difficulties and obstacles you've overcome. Consider all you have endured, coped with and survived in your life, be it loss, lack of opportunity or other adversities and hardships. What strengths or unique characteristics did you use to achieve your accomplishments and overcome adversity to get through hardships?

_____

_____

_____

_____

_____

_____

_____

_____

_____

_____

_____

_____

Write about what these adversities have taught you about yourself and your capabilities. Adversities have been found to make people mentally tougher and resilient.

_____

_____

_____

_____

_____

_____

_____

_____

_____

_____

_____

_____

_____

_____

_____

_____

Your superpowers

Circle five to ten character strengths below that you believe are your main strengths.

Appreciation of beauty and excellence	Bravery	Fairness
Creativity	Curiosity	Honesty
Forgiveness	Gratitude	Humour
Hope	Humility	Leadership
Judgement	Kindness	Perseverance
Love	Love of learning	Self-regulation
Perspective	Prudence	Teamwork
Social intelligence	Spirituality	Zest

Now visit viacharacter.org to take the 10-minute test to see your top five. Do they match with your own beliefs about your top five? Any surprises?

_____

_____

_____

_____

_____

_____

_____

_____

_____

_____

_____

_____

_____

_____

_____

Using your superpowers

Write down a problem you are currently wrangling with or a difficult situation you've been in. It could be struggling to maintain harmony in a relationship, financial or health issues, problems at work, something you're worrying about.

_____

_____

_____

_____

_____

_____

Which of your character strengths could you use to help you navigate the challenge you wrote about? Which people could you turn to?

_____

_____

_____

_____

_____

_____

Brainstorm ways you could use your character strengths more regularly in daily life.

_____

_____

_____

_____

_____

_____

_____

_____

_____

_____

_____

_____

_____

_____

_____

_____

Balance self-acceptance with self-improvement

To fully appreciate where and who you are now, as well as celebrating your strengths and developing an attitude of gratitude, you also need to accept your weaknesses. Only then can you feel ready to build on your strengths and improve areas that will enable your growth.

Write down what you think you are terrible at, or list your areas of weakness and some of your flaws/imperfections.

_____

_____

_____

_____

1. Put a smiley face next to those weaknesses or imperfections (on this page, above) to show you are now willing to accept these imperfections as part of you that you don't feel compelled to change or work on improving.

2. Circle those that you'd like to work on to improve and write below about how improving these will make you feel.

_____

_____

_____

_____

List the flaws and imperfections of the people you love/admire including your best friends and favourite characters from films and books. Aren't they endearing?

Review the list of your own flaws and imperfections on the previous page. Have you ever considered that these might be endearing too?

The self-judgement you may feel about your own imperfections doesn't remove your flaws; it just makes you feel bad about them. Your imperfections are part of you, and they are what make you human, relatable and likeable.

You don't love your best friends because of what their face or body looks like, or because they passed their exams, or have a good job. You love them for who they actually are, flaws and all. Isn't it time you extended yourself the same level of love and acceptance?

Achievement: growth

On one side of the page write down all that you are grateful to have in your life, all the stuff, people, achievements and experiences you're thankful for.

On the other side of the page write down all that you hope to have and achieve in your life, all the stuff, people, goals and experiences you hope to enjoy in the future.

GRATITUDE   **GOALS/GROWTH**

_____   _____

_____   _____

_____   _____

_____   _____

_____   _____

_____   _____

_____   _____

_____   _____

_____   _____

GRATITUDE

GOALS/GROWTH

Why do you want it?

Why do you want what you want? Consider the *why* behind the things/achievements/experiences in the right-hand list on pages 88–89 and what feeling achieving your goals or getting a new job/home/partner/qualification would give you. For example, make your family proud, boost your confidence, give you a feeling of security. Write about this below.

Now jot down what else you could do right now to feel those same feelings.

For example, if moving into your own home would make you feel comfy and warm, you could move your furniture around and buy some cushions and lighting to give you the same cosy space in the meantime.

Enjoy the journey

To feel like you are enough, you need to focus your time and attention on enjoying the journey as well as reaching a desired destination. This is why it's worth devoting time to enjoying the present as much as striving for what you want in the future.

Remember that what
you now have was once
among the things
you only hoped for.

EPICURUS

Goal setting

Write down small steps you can take to help you accomplish your goals. This way you'll feel like you are doing enough, even if that involves achieving one small thing each day or week, towards reaching your desired destination. By committing to regular intentional action you are focusing on devotion, rather than perfection.

Fill in this goal-setting pledge:

I aim to _____

_____

by _____

To get there I will complete the following small steps

_____

_____

_____

_____

_____

_____

_____

I will regularly reward myself with the following self-care treats

_____

_____

_____

_____

_____

_____

PART THREE

SELF

The most important relationship you have (and the most enduring) is the one you have with yourself. So far, we've focused on your self-worth as shaped by expectations, comparison with others and your perception of how other people see you and, consequently, how you see yourself. We've worked on developing curiosity and turning "compare and despair" into "compare and inspire". We've balanced gratitude and growth so you can enjoy your journey and appreciate what's good enough. Now it's time to go a little deeper so you can know you are enough once and for all.

Knowing you are enough as you are doesn't mean you stop learning, growing, improving or developing. Personal growth gives our lives meaning and makes us feel good. Our accomplishments embolden us, and help us to believe in our capabilities and reduce that imposter syndrome that can creep in and make us question our "enoughness", no matter how "well" we are doing in life or at work. As well as prompts to help boost your self-belief, self-compassion and self-love, in this section of the journal you'll also find prompts to help you learn from mistakes, forgive yourself and talk back to your inner critic, so you can keep going and keep growing. Because the way you speak to yourself and treat yourself is vital.

Are you ready for some deep introspection? It's time to work on your relationship with you!

Are you good enough to yourself?

Rather than wondering and worrying whether you are good enough, how about shifting your focus to being good enough to yourself? That's what self-compassion is all about.

You've already started on the journey to switch your thoughts from envy and inadequacy to inspiration, and have begun to replace judgement with curiosity – this is ongoing work, so let's build your self-compassion. First, accept that comparison is a natural default for our human brains, but be gentle with yourself when you find you are in "compare and despair" mode by running through kind affirmations, giving yourself permission to be imperfect and treating yourself like you would a good friend.

When we practise loving kindness and compassion, we are the first ones to profit.

RUMI

Honouring difficulty and the beauty of life

What makes you feel disappointed? For example, when you see people posting about their "soulmates" or "dream job" on social media, when you see other people sharing their achievements and wonder what you've done with your life.

_____

_____

_____

_____

_____

_____

What do you feel guilty or bad about? Write it down here.

_____

_____

_____

_____

_____

_____

These feelings are valid, so give yourself space to feel and honour them, but then remind yourself of the following truths by affirming the following statements. Say them out loud, or in your head if you prefer.

I have things and have accomplished things that other people would love to have/have achieved.

I am doing my best with what I have, and that is enough.

I already have so much to be grateful for.

I am a good person, living a life aligned with my values, and that is enough.

I am flawed and imperfect and so is everyone else. And that's what makes us beautiful.

Compassion affirmation

Copy out the following affirmations to build your self-compassion:

As long as I show up and do my best on any given day, that is enough.

_____

_____

_____

I accept that some days I may falter and that's okay. I give myself permission to be human.

_____

_____

_____

What other kind words of knowing might you offer yourself? Write them below.

_____

_____

_____

Use this space to write more compassionate affirmations.

_____

_____

_____

Proving your worth

Now jot down some proof (evidence of these affirmations). Gather proof from your achievements and gratitude list on page 76–79 and 88–89.

The "enoughness" equation

We've worked on accepting our flaws and understanding that nobody is perfect. Even those who seem brilliant at everything are usually not or those who seem to have it all actually don't. You likely have a characteristic or something in your life they wish they had.

The truth is, there will always be someone better, prettier, faster than you and there will always be room for improvement. You will always be an unfinished yet wonderful human who is and always will be a work in progress – and that is enough!

> **"Enoughness" = self-acceptance + self-belief + self-compassion**

Permission to be human

Write yourself a permission slip to be human below.

I (name) _____
give myself permission to be human. This means I accept that I may forget, stumble, fall or get angry. I might misunderstand or be misunderstood. I might say or do the wrong thing or show up in a way I'd rather not. This is part of the human experience and I am constantly learning. I give myself permission to be human.

I accept myself, I forgive myself, I believe in myself, I love myself.

I am good enough not despite the mistakes I make but *because* of them, because messing up is how I learn and grow.

Signed _____

Forgive your failures

Guilt or a feeling that we've done badly in the past can get in the way of our self-worth. Holding on to the past can make us feel bad about ourselves and stop us from moving forward – unless we practise forgiveness and learn lessons from our mistakes.

List your mistakes and failures here:

_____

_____

_____

_____

_____

_____

_____

_____

_____

_____

_____

_____

Failure equals feedback

We learn more from what we get wrong than from what we get right. So failures enable improvement and growth.

What did they teach you about what *not* to do next time? What will you do differently next time with the benefit of hindsight?

_____

_____

_____

_____

_____

What did your mistakes teach you about yourself?

_____

_____

_____

_____

_____

_____

_____

Guilt doesn't undo what you're feeling guilty about. We all mess up and say or do things we wish we hadn't because we're human. What advice would you give to a friend who's feeling guilty to help them feel better? Write it down below.

_____

_____

_____

_____

_____

_____

_____

_____

_____

_____

_____

_____

Forgive yourself

Write a letter of apology and forgiveness to get your feelings out.

I forgive myself for...

_____

_____

_____

_____

_____

Now write a note of reassurance. For example: "I was young and didn't think properly. I now know how to respond better. The way I would handle this differently in future would be to..."

_____

_____

_____

_____

_____

Yay! You've learned from this. It's time to let go and move on.

Make peace with yourself

Write a letter to your body.

For example, "Dear body, I promise to stop hating you because you're the only one I've got. You help me do what I need to do in my daily life. You're keeping me alive. You're great at protecting me. You're amazing!"

_____

_____

_____

_____

_____

_____

_____

_____

_____

_____

_____

Healing words

Use this space to write down any other words of forgiveness to release anything you are holding on to that is stopping you from moving forward and feeling good enough.

_____

_____

_____

_____

_____

_____

_____

_____

_____

_____

_____

_____

_____

_____

_____

_____

Boost your belief in you!

Recollect instances of times you've done something you didn't think you could, when you've performed better and/or done better than you thought you might at something. Write about those times below.

What do these experiences tell you about yourself? For example, the time you stood up in front of a room of people to deliver a presentation means you are brave. Joining a new team or trying something new when you felt uncomfortable means you can do hard things and rise to challenges.

Create a list of positive "I ams" and "I cans" – all evidence that you are good enough as you are and that your willingness to grow is simply a bonus.

I am...

_____

_____

because...

_____

_____

I can...

_____

_____

Beat imposter syndrome

Imposter syndrome is the feeling that we don't deserve the success, job or opportunity we've been given because we're just not good enough. Even the highest-achieving people feel it. It's the feeling that you're about to be found out as an imposter. List examples of when you feel like an imposter below.

_____

_____

_____

_____

_____

_____

_____

_____

_____

_____

_____

_____

_____

List the reasons why you deserve to do what you do. For example, why you were hired, invited to speak in public, etc. What did the person hiring or inviting you to do this thing that is triggering imposter syndrome recognize in you?

_____

_____

_____

_____

_____

_____

_____

_____

_____

_____

_____

_____

_____

_____

_____

_____

Pat on the back

What have you done right or well at work recently?

_____

_____

_____

_____

_____

_____

What have you done right or well in other areas where you may feel like an imposter – as if you are going to get found out at any moment?

_____

_____

_____

_____

_____

_____

Remind yourself nobody else has it all together either and most people feel like an imposter from time to time.

List the parts of your life under your control that have been shaped by your own choices, decisions and actions. Write down anything that has happened because of your own abilities, intelligence and efforts. Now own them. Feel proud!

_____

_____

_____

_____

_____

_____

_____

_____

_____

_____

_____

_____

_____

_____

_____

Praise you

Use this space to jot down any compliments or praise you've received. This is useful for remembering not just your "enoughness" but your awesomeness too.

_____

_____

_____

_____

These pieces of evidence can help counter the negative feedback we give ourselves. Now finish the following sentences:

I deserve to feel good about myself because...

_____

_____

_____

_____

I deserve to achieve my dreams because...

_____

_____

_____

_____

A reminder

Remember your brain has been trained to ignore all the things you're doing well because those things don't pose a threat to you. It focuses on your weaker points because that could lead to failure or rejection. Your inner critic has your best interests at heart, and is trying to prevent rejection and protect you from shame or embarrassment. But criticism is not the way to get the best out of someone; compassion and encouragement are far more motivating.

Counter the critic

Write down things your critical voice will tell you that you're doing wrong or badly.

_____

_____

_____

_____

_____

_____

Now counter that voice with something you've done well.

_____

_____

_____

_____

_____

_____

Has your negativity bias – the inner wiring that causes us to focus on what has or what might go wrong to protect us from harm (also known as your inner critic or imposter syndrome) – stopped you from trying something you might enjoy? Write about this below.

Talk back to your inner critic

Notice your mind chatter. This is important because it is often overtly and unfairly negative as well as inaccurate and inflexible. Tune in to any automatic negative thoughts (ANTs) that crop up throughout the day. Often these thoughts begin with, "They think I'm...", "I'm so...".

Today, my ANTs included:

_____

_____

_____

_____

_____

_____

_____

_____

_____

_____

_____

_____

_____

What do you tend to judge yourself critically about? Write your most frequent criticisms here.

_____

_____

_____

_____

_____

_____

_____

_____

_____

_____

_____

_____

_____

_____

_____

_____

Critical analysis

Are there any themes or categories these criticisms tend to fall into? For example, parenting, friendships and other relationships, work, body image, self-care, reliability? Jot them down below.

Are there any patterns your critical voice follows? For example, you might find your self-critic is louder after being around certain people, in certain environments, after you've been in certain situations.

_____

_____

_____

_____

_____

_____

_____

_____

_____

_____

_____

_____

_____

_____

Take your thoughts to court

Call your inner critic to the stand. Seek evidence to dispute the criticisms you've listed – you'll reframe them with more accurate and flexible thoughts that better serve you on the next pages.

Critical thought #1

_____

_____

_____

_____

Write down evidence to support or dispute that thought. You only need to find one small shred of evidence to counter a thought to be able to reframe it.

_____

_____

_____

_____

Critical thought #2

_____

_____

_____

_____

Evidence to dispute that thought

_____

_____

_____

_____

Critical thought #3

_____

_____

_____

_____

Evidence to dispute that thought

_____

_____

_____

Reframe unhelpful thoughts

Based on the evidence you've found, ask yourself: What's another way of looking at this? For example, you could reframe "I always say the wrong thing" with "I do sometimes say the wrong thing, but I also say the right thing a lot too. I just don't notice those times. I'm working on pausing before I respond, so well done me."

Reframe another thought here. For example, reframe the thought "You don't deserve a promotion at work, you're not good enough" with "I am worthy enough to apply for the promotion – my boss has been impressed with my work recently and I have the skills that are needed, so it's worth a try."

Your turn...

_____

_____

_____

_____

_____

_____

_____

_____

_____

_____

_____

_____

Write down some things you'd like to say to your own inner critic. For example: "Thanks for trying to protect me but you're going about it the wrong way and it's making me feel bad. I'll take it from here."

_____

_____

_____

_____

_____

_____

_____

_____

_____

_____

_____

_____

_____

_____

Naysayer vs yaysayer

Replace your inner critic with an inner cheerleader. What might they have to say about certain situations? Instead of berating you for not getting as much done today as you'd hoped, your inner cheerleader might say, "Well done for getting three things done, that's progress." Refer back to your compassionate affirmations on page 102 if you need a prompt.

Rewrite your stories and "enoughness" narrative

Revisit the expectations section on pages 12–20 and see what you were saying about yourself at the beginning of this workbook. Can you reframe that self-judgement by getting curious about another way of looking at it? For example, replace, "I'm too sensitive" with "Sensitivity is a superpower. It means I care deeply and know what I do and don't want. It's a strength, not a weakness."

Write reframes to your previous stories and "enoughness" narrative below.

_____

_____

_____

_____

_____

_____

_____

_____

_____

_____

Befriend yourself

Imagine a child or your best friend was beating themselves up and feeling bad, criticizing themselves by saying the words you've written here. Picture them being upset. What would you say to comfort them? Write it down here.

_____

_____

_____

_____

_____

_____

_____

_____

_____

_____

_____

_____

_____

_____

_____

What supportive actions can you take next time you make a mistake/fail/do or say something that you might judge or criticize yourself for? Could you offer yourself reassurance, a cup of tea, a chat with a friend, a walk in nature, a yoga session or a shower? List your ideas here.

_____

_____

_____

_____

_____

_____

_____

_____

_____

_____

_____

_____

_____

_____

Cheery prompts to counter the critical voice

List of delight

Become a joy detective and find the good in the ordinary day to day. Make a list of all the tiny things that bring you a sense of delight – from the smell of coffee in the morning to the softness of a book page, and the taste of a fresh strawberry to the sound of birdsong outside your window. Remember these tiny delights whenever you're feeling bad about yourself to shift your perspective. You could make your list of delight in your phone's notes and refer to it whenever you need a boost.

_____

_____

_____

_____

_____

_____

_____

_____

_____

_____

_____

Silver-lining list

Find the good in a bad situation and consider alternative ways of looking at it. For example, if someone is getting you down, think about the people in your life who lift you up. Perhaps someone rarely expresses their appreciation to you in words, but they show you via their actions. Write down some silver linings here.

_____

_____

_____

_____

_____

Kindness brainstorm

Kindness is one of the most effective inducers of positive emotion – a great counter to the negativity bias. List ideas for kind acts to enable you to get a "giver's glow". For example, delivering daffodils to friends, sellotaping a few coins on a parking meter or donating clothes to charity.

_____

_____

_____

_____

_____

Self-approval and self-love

Now you've pulled out the weeds and planted new seeds that better serve you. Affirm those positive thoughts by writing them as statements below.

I am lovable   **I am a good person**

I am deserving of respect

I am skilled

I am trying my best

I am learning from my mistakes

I am more capable   **I have so much to**
than I thought   **be grateful for**

I am good at...   **With effort I can**
                                    get better at...

I am enough

Your turn:

I am...

_____

_____

_____

Love yourself

What if you saw yourself through the eyes of someone who believes in you, someone who admires you and sees your potential and possibilities? What are the best bits about you? If you need help with this, ask people close to you what they think. Write yourself a love letter giving 20 reasons why you love who you are.

Dear Me,

I love you because:

1. _____

_____

_____

2. _____

_____

_____

3. _____

_____

_____

4. _____

_____

_____

5.

6.

7.

8.

9.

10.

CONCLUSION

In the story of your life, you can be your own best ally or your own worst enemy. There are many external directors who can dictate the roles you play based on their own expectations and "shoulds". Yet only you have the power to rewrite the script and become the author of your own story, controlling the plot as it unfolds.

In a fast-paced world of perpetual pressure to strive and live your "best life", it can be difficult to strike a healthy balance between growth and gratitude, self-improvement and self-acceptance, betterment and contentment. For this reason, it's important to centre yourself with compassionate curiosity, question the expectations placed on you, talk back to your inner critic and give your inner cheerleader ample airtime.

The aim is to be your true self rather than the person you think you should be to fit in or impress others. This becomes easier when you question, with gentle curiosity, the judgemental thoughts you've internalized over time, and build awareness about what leads you to think and feel the way you do.

Only when you grow your self-acceptance, self-belief and self-compassion can you really see, value and approve of yourself as you truly are – a unique, worthy, valuable individual, deserving of a life in which you can flourish.

RESOURCES AND FURTHER READING

Websites

Find and develop your character strengths –
www.viacharacter.org/character-strengths

Self-compassion exercises –
www.self-compassion.org/category/exercises/#exercises

Young Minds mental health support to help
young people have the resilience to overcome
life's challenges – www.youngminds.org.uk

MIND mental health charity – www.mind.org.uk

The Samaritans; whatever you're going through, a
Samaritan will go through it with you. Call 116 123 for
free, anytime, all year round – www.samaritans.org

Find out about volunteering opportunities –
www.dofe.org/thelatest/volunteering-ideas

Ideas for acts of kindness –
www.kindnessuk.com/acts_of_kindness.php

Books

Tara Brach, *Radical Acceptance: Embracing Your Life With the Heart of a Buddha* (2003, Bantam)

Tara Brach, *Radical Compassion* (2020, Penguin)

Brené Brown, *The Gifts of Imperfection* (2020, Hazelden)

Glennon Doyle, *Untamed: Stop Pleasing, Start Living* (2020, Vermilion)

Adam Grant, *Originals: How Non-Conformists Move The World* (2016, W. H. Allen)

Louise L. Hay, *You Can Heal Your Life* (1984, Hay House)

Alicia Keys, *More Myself: A Journey* (2020, Macmillan)

Kristin Nell, *Self-Compassion: The Proven Power of Being Kind to Yourself* (2011, William Morrow)

Jennifer Pastiloff, *On Being Human: A Memoir of Waking Up, Living Real, and Listening Hard* (2019, John Murray Learning)

Cheryl Rickman, *The Happiness Bible: The Definitive Guide for Sustainable Wellbeing* (2019, Octopus)

Cheryl Rickman, *Navigating Loneliness: How to Connect With Yourself and Others – A Mental Health Handbook* (2021, Trigger Publishing)

Cheryl Rickman, *You Are Enough* (2021, Vie)

Jen Sincero, *You Are a Badass: How to Stop Doubting Your Greatness and Start Living an Awesome Life* (2016, John Murray Learning)

Bronnie Ware, *The Top Five Regrets of the Dying: A Life Transformed by the Dearly Departed* (2012, Hay House UK)

ABOUT THE AUTHOR

Cheryl Rickman is a *Sunday Times* bestselling author, a ghostwriter of 27 self-help, well-being and business books and a Positive Psychology Practitioner. She specializes in writing empowering, practical books to help people fret less and flourish more. Her most recent books include *You Can Flourish*, *Tree Glee* and *Navigating Loneliness*. She lives in the English countryside with her partner James, daughter Brooke and their two Labradors.

ALSO BY CHERYL RICKMAN

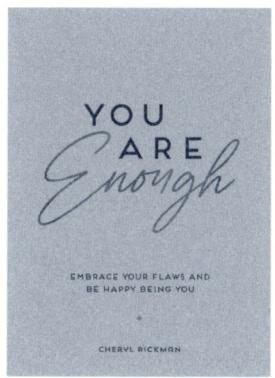

You Are Enough

Embrace Your Flaws and Be Happy Being You

978-1-80007-002-8

Have you ever experienced imposter syndrome? Do you often find yourself seeking approval from others? Is beating yourself up getting you down? Then this book can help you.

With thought-provoking advice, a step-by-step action plan and a simple method to challenge your inner critic, *You Are Enough* will help you embrace your flaws and celebrate your unique awesomeness. Let go of the myth of perfection, finally stop comparing yourself to others, and learn how to be happy with all that you are.

You Can Flourish

A Wellness Workbook to Help You Thrive and Feel Your Best

978-1-80007-681-5

Learn how to fret less and flourish more with this empowering guidebook, filled with helpful advice and practical exercises to boost your well-being and balance life's ups and downs.

Feeling better isn't always about feeling good. It's about feeling it all – happiness, sadness and everything in between. In *You Can Flourish*, Positive Psychology Practitioner Cheryl Rickman takes you step by step through simple exercises to help you better experience both the positive and negative in life, so you can thrive and grow.

Have you enjoyed this book?

If so, why not write a review on your favourite website?

If you're interested in finding out more about our books,
find us on Facebook at **Summersdale Publishers**, on Twitter/X
at **@Summersdale** and on Instagram and TikTok at
@summersdalebooks and get in touch.
We'd love to hear from you!

Thanks very much for buying this Summersdale book.

www.summersdale.com